Gladys Kidd

Small Business Playing Big:

The Game of Government Contracting

Small Business Playing Big:
The Game of Government Contracting

A business book, providing techniques, strategies
and lessons learned working in the public sector arena.

By Gladys Kidd, Author and President & CEO
Gladys Kidd & Associates, Inc. a South Florida based firm.

Published by: Kidd, Ammons, LLC
P. O. Box 908, Lake Worth, FL 33460

First Edition, June, 2012
Published in the United States

ISBN-13: 978-1468147070

ISBN-10: 1468147072

Book cover and text design:
Huntley Burgher & Associates, Inc.

"The big secret in life is that there is no big secret. Whatever your goal, you can get there if you're willing to work."

Oprah Winfrey, O Magazine

CONTENTS

ACKNOWLEDGEMENTS

There are many people throughout my career that need to be acknowledged and thanked including:

My parents who inspired me with their limited resources to always think big.

All the professional women who I saw growing up that gave me something to dream about.

My mentors, Harold Wolfson and Nikki Beare, who believed in me and gave me the opportunity to grow

My friends Brenda Howard and Magdalena Graham who were two fearless black women that showed me how to fly.

Brenda was never afraid to express her mind without reservations. Her favorite saying was that she was bloody but unbowed. She earned her respect and taught me how to stand up for myself and for what was right.

Magdalena was always an entrepreneur who taught me how to multitask. She moved on to New Mexico to pursue a successful career in real estate. When people would question her earlier in her career about how she could attend college at night and manage her family needs, she would always point out that a stove had four burners and an oven and that on Sundays, when everyone else was watching tv, she would cook and package meals for the week which allowed her to further her education.

It has been my good fortune to work with some of the greatest professionals in the transportation industry. What a great group of people and inspiring atmosphere to work. And to those who played games, you know who you are, I wish you well. You just can't keep a good woman down.

Thanks too to my team of editors from CreateSpace who guided me with the tone and style of the book and to my friends who helped me with the manuscript including Magdalena Graham, Adrienne McBeth, Patricia "Tish" Burgher, and my daughter Jacqueline Kidd.

Special thanks to my husband, Herb Ammons, who provided technical support, who was my editor, advisor, and all around troubleshooter and make it happen person. I thank him for being my better half for the past 32 years. Behind every great woman there is a strong man to pick her up should she fall and to push her forward should she despair.

I would like to inspire my grandson, Christopher Kidd Johnson, who has been bitten by the entrepreneurial bug. My advice to him is to follow his bliss and the advice I share in the book. This book is dedicated to you.

And last but not least, I would like to thank the Lord from whom all blessings flow. Thanks for allowing me to realize early in my career that all things are possible if God is on your side and for helping me to achieve my dreams.

ABOUT THE AUTHOR

Gladys Kidd owned and operated Gladys Kidd and Associates, a public relations and marketing firm, in Miami for almost three decades.

She started with limited resources, had to overcome numerous challenges, and her achievements were due to hard work and a strong personality. She is well known for her work in the public transportation industry in South Florida.

Her mother contributed to her entrepreneurial spirit. Being the only female of four children, she wanted to make sure that her daughter had the right preparation. Gladys attended one of Panama's best private business schools.

In her new book, "Small Business Playing Big: The Game of Government Contracting," she shares basic techniques and strategies of operating a business, and discusses important lessons learned in winning and managing government contracts.

Today, Ms. Kidd is a savvy businesswoman involved in several projects. In 2010, she published "Hope for Tomorrow, A Book of Motivational Quotes" the first of a series of books that provide readers with optimism and inspiration.

The Panamanian native, arrived in Miami from New York in 1978 to work for Southeast Bank. Two years later, she began working for the newly formed Miami Dade County Tourism Department as cultural and special events manager. She was a grants administrator to fund cultural and special events and the liaison between the Council of

Arts & Sciences (now Cultural Affairs Council) and the Miami Dade Tourism Bureau (now the Greater Miami Convention and Visitors Bureau. Later, she worked in the sales and marketing department of the bureau and for the Sheraton Brickell Point Hotel.

Ms. Kidd has never forgotten where she began or the people that helped her along the path. She believes in giving back to the community. In 2003, the firm managed a community awareness campaign aimed at the victims of domestic violence and sexual abuse, including a television series "Silence Isn't Golden: Tell Somebody," that aired on public television. She has served on many local community boards, including the United Way, Cultural Affairs Council, and the Greater Miami Convention and Visitors Bureau.

Through the years, Ms. Kidd has found strength and inspiration from others who have succeeded in making their dreams come true through hard work and perseverance. The final section of the book offers quotations from successful men and women designed to inspire confidence and optimism.

FOREWORD

This book "Small Business Playing Big: The Game of Government Contracting" is not a traditional how-to book. It shares the author's techniques and strategies developed over almost three decades of running a business and offers advice about important lessons learned. The book is for novice and experienced managers who want to access the government marketplace and win small business contracts.

Topics Covered in the Book:

- Resources to start your business
- "No" is also an answer
- Bidding on government contracts
- Negotiating and collecting fees
- Bidding as a prime contractor
- Being a sub-consultant
- Forming a joint venture
- Marketing for competitive advantage
- Making effective presentations
- Documenting reports
- Making money and succeeding

I'd like to encourage those with the passion, the determination, and above all, the dream of owning their own business. In today's economy it could become more than a dream. It could become a neccesity. All things are possible, so think big. You must be willing to be disciplined and make the necessary sacrifices. I would like to mention here one of my favorite quotes by Vince Lombardi to inspire you:

"We would accomplish many more things if we did not think of them as impossible."

Small business today is Big Business! Small businesses contribute to the growth of the economy by employing people, purchasing goods and services, and paying taxes. Yet they are seldom given their due. When the economy suffers, they are the first to feel the cuts, and survival becomes a day-to-day matter.

Our economy is dependent on the continued growth and development of small businesses. With the Internet's new and developing technology, it is becoming easier for new entrepreneurs to use their creativity to make their mark in the new millennium.

Good luck.

Gladys Kidd, President and CEO
Gladys Kidd and Associates, Inc.

SECTION 1

Success is the best revenge

Success in business is never automatic, nor is it strictly based on luck (although a little never hurts). It depends on a lot of things, mostly the owner's foresight and organizational and problem-solving skills. A little "street smarts" or common sense never hurts, either. Starting a business is risky, and the chances of success are slim.

I believe that achieving excellence is being able to perform at a high level over a long period of time. In my case, I ran a business for almost three decades, a fact almost unheard of, given the failure of most small businesses. According to the U.S. Small Business Admin-istration, roughly 50 percent of small businesses fail within the first five years. Given my record, I believe I have achieved success. For small businesses, success is measured in terms of survival. It's every man and woman for him or herself and survival of the fittest.

My early training days in New York working for a major public rela-tions firm had set the stage. Upon arriving in Miami in 1978, this experience was complemented by positions in the banking, tourism, and hospitality industries, which gave me the tools, the experience, and the resources to venture out on my own.

Success is also about being in the right place at the right time. For me, the right place was Miami. During the '80s, diversity became the buzzword with federal, state, and local governments enacting ordinances requiring the utilization of minority businesses: women, blacks, Hispanics, and other minority groups.

Well, I had it made. I was diverse in many ways: black, female, and

Hispanic. We needed one more stripe to earn our wings as a "Perfect Minority" designation: A Jewish husband would have made me a Black/Female/Hispanic/Jewish minority contractor.

Another plus was the Transportation Equity Act for the 21st Century, (TEA-21), which built on ISTEA, The Intermodal Surface Transportation Efficiency Act (enacted in 1991), that mandated proactive public involvement at every stage of project planning and implementation affecting transportation projects. The Act required input and feedback from the public in order to build consensus before a project could be funded.

Being in the public relations business, we were in a position to develop our niche. We obtained all the necessary certifications as a minority firm, and we could offer public involvement services in English, Spanish, and Creole to address the county's multilingual communities.

The money you make measures success. As a business owner, I did not make all the money to be made, but I did well financially and invested wisely. However, what I accomplished was more than just making money. Success is also measured by the opportunity I afforded myself when I took that entrepreneurial plunge.

I created the opportunity to meet and work with some of the area's top professionals in the transportation industry, and I built many friendships and business relationships. From the beginning, I was an outsider to the male dominated industry. The firms working in this arena were mostly big players, with local and national reputations. However, as a small business, we built a bridge to the opportunities that were available and were able to play in the big league.

I especially enjoyed the ride, the challenge of the team spirit, the excitement of the bidding process to get new work, the creativity involved in preparing presentations, learning new things associated with the various projects, and usually being one of the only female members of the team.

It was clear early in the game that, as a small business, it was going to be difficult to land million-dollar contracts. However, there was nothing stopping us from getting four contracts of $250,000, thus a million dollars. So we were realistic starting out. You don't have to be a genius to figure out how to make a million dollars—or many millions, if that is your goal.

However, making money should be everyone's right. Start with the knowledge that we live in an abundant universe. My spiritual side led me to believe that the power of the universe would take care of me. I always envisioned myself surrounded by wealth and abundance.

I lived in the flight path of the Miami International Airport and near the Port of Miami, two of the area's largest economic engines, with millions of dollars and thousands of people flowing thru daily. My goal was to spiritually tap into that economic flow and energy. I started out small, but by growing my business, my billings went from $1,000 to $10,000 to $100,000. You get the picture.

Gratitude and appreciation are important elements of the equation, as well. You must truly be thankful for your blessings, instead of complaining about what other people have.

Family and friends may share your dream of running a business and offer encouragement and support. Just remember it is your dream.

Your competition will try to discredit you, but that is the nature of the beast. They will pull rank on you: they have more political allies and friends. They will question your ethnicity, your qualifications, your capabilities. They will play dirty.

However, if these were the only arguments they had, then I was winning. In the final analysis, the only thing that is truly important is how your clients remember you. "Let my record speak for itself."

SECTION 2

Don't let others define you. Define yourself!

In Miami, I was sort of an anomaly. People always tried to define me. Some thought I was Bahamian, Jamaican, Cuban - everything but Panamanian.

Some people would guess that, because I spoke English perfectly, I was not Hispanic. Others felt that, since I was Hispanic by birth, I could not be considered black. There was always that quandary whether I was black or Hispanic. But guess what? I can be black and Hispanic, too!

I have always known who I am. I am the daughter of proud West Indian parents who went to Panama to help build the Panama Canal. My ancestors had an enterprising spirit when they left their country for job opportunities in Panama. They had strong minds and bodies that conquered the rocks and the lakes that paved the path for the canal.

The Panama Canal, begun by France and completed by the United States, is one of the greatest architectural wonders of the world. It took nearly half a century to build.

I was raised in the African/West Indian/Panamanian/American cultural experience, influenced by their customs, languages, money, and foods.

All members of the black race came from Africa, so their customs and traditions are similar in many ways. I was schooled in both English and Spanish. I grew up absorbing the Hispanic culture, which was all around me as a child and teenager. Because of my skin color, upbringing, and personal choice, I always felt more black than Hispanic.

The point is that everything begins with a decision, and I decided to be in charge of my own reality. I figured out early on that, if I didn't define myself, plenty of folks would attempt to do so for me. I did not trust them to have my best interest in mind.

I also enjoy playing games with my Spanish, simply because I can. People see my skin color and don't know that I speak Spanish, and they have made derogatory comments in my presence because they thought I did not understand. They are stunned when I respond in Spanish. The truth is that Spanish is the universal language in Miami and, if you speak it, you are accepted. Miami is an international city represented by every country in Central and Latin America.

I have always been a good storyteller and developed my love for the English language from my father, who was employed by the U. S. Government in Panama.

When I was about eight, he would sit me on his lap and say, "Give me a four-letter word for caring," and I would quickly reply "love," to which he would proclaim, "Give that young lady a prize for being correct." I would beam with pride and read and study more for the next session. I also remembered going to work with him on the "Take your daughter to work day." I had a great role model in my dad. My father had a very competitive spirit and became one of Panama's top weightlifting champions representing his country at various competitions.

My mother contributed to my entrepreneurial spirit. Being the only female of four children, she wanted to make sure that I was well prepared for the world. She sent me to one of Panama's best private business schools to make sure that I had a solid foundation.

My mother was a seamstress and designed women's clothing. I learned early from her how important it is to run your own business and earn your own money. She hung a plaque in the dining room that read, "Give a man a fish and he eats for a day; teach a man to fish and he eats for a lifetime." Even from a young age, I read and absorbed that thought daily and it motivated me.

Another area over which you exercise a lot of control is your image. They say that you have one opportunity to make a good "first" impression. People will always remember you or try to forget you.

My reputation preceded me, mostly because I was different. I always loved clothes and learned early in my career that there is an art to dressing, which allows you to develop your own style. You don't have to run with the masses. You are not a one-size-fits-all type of person. Once you find the right formula, stick with it.

Your image is important in business. Invest in quality pieces for your wardrobe. Emulate the style of professional women (and men) whom you admire. Always dress in a professional manner, making sure to be properly groomed. Remember, you must play the part to be the boss—a rule that's otherwise known as "Fake it until you make it."

SECTION 3

Starting and operating a business

Chapter 1: The Entrepreneurial Plunge

After several jobs in the public and private sectors, I made the decision to start my own company. I had made excellent contacts, had gotten married, and had a host of mentors that provided encouragement. A big motivator was the knowledge that minority public relations and marketing firms were limited, although the Hispanic community had started to actively enter the market.

After overcoming my fears and carefully evaluating the entrepreneurial plunge with friends and family, I decided to make a go of it. I decided to enter the field as a consultant.

I started my business in the bedroom of my home, armed with a computer and lots of guts. I always advise people to start where they are. If you wait to get everything perfect, exactly the way you want it, then you probably will be waiting a long time.

I liken it to stepping into the flow of prosperity. If you are not "in the stream" very little can happen. So, I decided to be courageous and step off the sidewalk into the stream where the money flows. To women, I say that I now realize that running a business is similar in some respects to running a household: researching, planning, executing, and paying bills. Women do that every day.

After working on lots of small projects when we got started, we eventually moved up to handling larger projects. In 1988, when the Florida Lottery was introduced, we were among the first contractors to assist in recruiting retailers to sell Lottery products.

Our first major project was the City of Miami Southeast Overtown Park West Redevelopment project to build affordable housing in Overtown, a historic African American community located in the central business district of downtown Miami. Since Overtown is a minority community, the city hired a minority firm to help them promote the project.

My mentor, Nikki Beare, an established public relations consultant, and a leader championing the crusade for more women and minorities to get their share of contracts, convinced me that she would help me put together a team and go after the bid. We formed a joint venture and won the $150,000 contract.

I still remember the feeling I experienced when we won our first major contract. It was the largest sum we had ever been awarded, and some people felt that we had made it for life. The reality was that, after salaries, rent, and expenses, it was just enough to keep us in the game. We were very proud because it was our first public service contract that could lead to bigger and better things.

Chapter 2: No Is Also an Answer

A lifelong motto of mine has been "No is also an answer." It is interesting to see how people react when you say "no" and how you react when "no" is said to you. Being a business owner will provide many opportunities for you to say and hear the word "no." Get used to it and understand when it is necessary to say it and appreciate what is happening when it is being said to you. That does not mean that you must be defeated. You probably will hear "no" more often than "yes."

Conversely, you must learn to say no in situations that don't benefit your agenda or profitability. Don't allow yourself to be set up to fail. You must be selective when it comes to choosing a partner and how much and when they pay you. You must know your scope of services, your deadlines, and whether you have sufficient time to complete tasks on time and within budget. Don't oversell yourself. If you don't have the capabilities to complete all the tasks, make sure you hire experienced professionals to fill those roles.

As a minority business owner, I always hated the term minority, but I wore it like a badge because it was the tool that enabled me to survive in my line of work. I always told people that there was nothing "minor" about me. I am almost six feet tall, full-bodied, full-bosomed, intelligent, well-read, and well-traveled, with a big heart, a big voice, and big ideas. I walk the walk and talk the talk. And as one of my mentors told me early in my career, "Money talks, and bull— walks." It is a basic principle that has guided me throughout my life.

During the time I ran my business, I realized that the services we provided were not as important as the skills of other professionals on the team. However, our services were required by law and important to the process. Organizers of many publicly funded projects must solicit community input and seek consensus before the money will flow. Therefore, our team was always included and treated with the utmost respect.

I had the opportunity to work on several teams, covering a variety of transportation and capital improvement projects during the design and construction phases. I met and worked with some of South Florida's leading architects, engineers, urban planners, landscapers, environmentalists, and other professionals in the industry. This was a very privileged place. Working and learning different aspects of the industry from these top professionals was an ever-flowing fountain of knowledge.

The first rule was to conduct business the professional way. There are still many so-called business people that spend most of their time at city or county halls kissing up to politicians, shaking them down for contracts.

The truth is that politicians come and politicians go, and the one who is your friend today could be your enemy tomorrow. Nothing in life is free, so sooner or later, if you go that route, you will have to pay the piper. You really can maintain minimum contact and survive.

Instead, I spent more time building alliances that would potentially lead to teaming opportunities with larger companies that currently had large contracts or that were bidding on large contracts. Most contracts required the inclusion of a Disadvantaged Business Enterprise (DBE) or a Minority Business Enterprise (MBE), two designations we held.

We promoted the fact that we were a minority firm. The idea was to get known for the type of services we provided and to get included when they put their team together to bid on major contracts.

Our firm was actively recruited. As a matter of fact, after we began working on different projects, word got around, and sometimes, we would end up competing on more than one team. It is great to have a good reputation.

Joining more than one team can be tricky, however. You must let all the competing teams know of your involvement with the other teams. This way, if they have any propriety information or secret strategic plan they want to protect, then your firm will not be included in those discussions.

Actually, it was not hard for our company to end up on more than one competing team. There was little or no competition from other companies for these types of contracts. Most other firms were either not certified or did not have the experience and track record.

The rationale for pursuing government contracts was that there was a lot more money to be made compared to the private sector. The flipside of that is the application and renewal process which used to be very time consuming. Some renewals are done on an annual basis. In addition each agency had their own certification process. Currently the process has been simplified from the earlier days, but it still requires a lot of paperwork.

Chapter 3: A Toolbox Of Tips For Small Businesses

When you start a business, there are no guarantees as to whether you will succeed or fail. But for the right person, the advantages outweigh the risks. Resources are available to help you start, grow, and succeed.

Many small businesses succeed because of timing and luck. However, to sustain your growth, you will need to have a solid plan, discipline, and strong problem-solving skills. If you concentrate on making money and managing your cash flow, you should be able to grow a very healthy business for the long run.

Here are basic rules to apply in running and operating a small, minority-owned business:

A. Be Prepared

It is important to know how to prepare a business plan, proposals, budgets, etc. You must have good planning skills; and also be able to properly organize your time and follow through on details. You must know how to put the right team of people together who share your values and goals. But, mostly, you must have courage and be disciplined.

Too many people believe that starting a business means there is no accountability. They view the money they make as their own personal money. Others feel that owning a business means they do not have to work. Quite the contrary, most small-business owners are used to twelve-hour days.

Others begin their businesses without being adequately prepared and give up far too quickly, after a few rejections or when they realize that people are not lining up to do business with them. But most small businesses will get more "nos" than positive responses. You must develop a thick skin; let the rejections bounce off your back and push ahead.

You also need strong determination to find ways to overcome all the challenges and surprises that you will encounter.

B. Setting Up A Home-Based Business

Setting up a home-based business may be a more cost-effective alternative when you are getting started.

First, research the type of business you want to establish. Find out what licensing and zoning requirements you must meet, and ensure that you meet them all. Do not cut corners here because it could come back to haunt you.

Having a home-based business, you need to set aside a particular place in your home for your business. Make sure the space is large enough and that you have appropriate electrical outlets.

Install a business phone separate from your residential line. Install an answering machine to take calls when you are out or occupied. Make sure you have a professional recording that announces your business. Hold client meetings in rented conference rooms or set business meetings in restaurants.

You should develop a logo and a slogan for your company. Invest in quality stationery and prepare a marketing package that includes a description of your business, capabilities, background, and clients served. Also include your address, telephone number, e-mail, and website. Use a businesslike, professional email address, not your personal "LadyBug, LoverBoy" type address. The marketing package should be distributed to both present and prospective clients.

C. Planning

It has been said that if you fail to plan, then you plan to fail. Plan your organizational structure, strategy, staffing, and marketing. You may find it helpful to have a small-business consultant or your accountant to help you.

At the beginning, you may want to use independent contractors, rather than have full-time employees. You may not have enough work to warrant full-time employees. You can negotiate fees with independent contractors to handle some of the work at fixed rates. The advantage is that you do not have payroll and the expense of payroll taxes.

Are you planning to run a service business, such as public relations? During your planning phase, you must decide what sets your firm apart from the rest. All companies feel that they are good, but basically we more or less all do the same things. However, developing a niche is important to make you stand out.

What sets your firm apart from the rest? What areas do you want to develop as your specialty? After all, you cannot be all things to all people. For what do you want to be known? Our specialty was public involvement, supporting transportation and infrastructure-improvement projects. Our niche was that we marketed ourselves as multi-disciplinary and multi-lingual. If you try to be master of all trades, people will not take you seriously.

Product development falls under proper planning. With the advent of the Internet, everyone has a product to sell. We all have lots of ideas and we want to capitalize on them. However, there is no easy way to introduce a product to market. If you try to short-circuit the process, it could cost you dearly. Everything has a beginning, a middle, and an end. If you eliminate one of those steps you may not succeed.

You must have patience, do your homework, research the concept, see if anyone else has a similar product, test the product, and do more research before you attempt to go to market. The Internet is a wonderful source of information that can help you. If you don't follow the process, you will end up with an ill-conceived idea that only you believe in.

D. Getting Capital

You need money to grow a business, to purchase or replace equipment, or to cover other expenses. There are many sources to consider: personal savings, credit cards, a business credit line, and a business check card, a second mortgage on your home, cashing in on your insurance policy or a company profit-sharing plan, borrowing from friends and family, or getting a business loan.

No business plan, no loan. Your business plan doesn't have to be formal, but it must be well thought out. Small businesses seeking loans should know how to prepare the kind of business plans that banks require. Lenders scrutinize specific points, and applicants should tailor their submittal accordingly. You can get help from the Small Business Administration and other small-business resources.

A business plan should include a description of your business' physical location, facilities and equipment, kinds of employees needed, inventory requirements and suppliers, and any other applicable operating, management, marketing and financial details. The plan should focus on the bank's concern with reducing risks and the applicant's ability to repay the loan.

To justify the loan, you should be able to show the bank how the business intends to use the money and how viable your plan is. Loan applicants should also first establish a strong relationship with the lending bank to increase the possibility of having a loan approved.

Getting capital will be vitally important to your survival. Getting yourself set up with a Dunn and Bradstreet number, a business-specific credit card, and other credit-building assets is important.

Money is also needed to cover contract expenses. Some contracts require you to incur expenses from third parties who work only on a cash basis. So, if you do not have the resources to pay your bills, you are going to be out of business quickly.

In running your business, the most important rule is about making and spending money. If you can pay your bills, then you are alive. If you are alive, you can survive. Your suppliers are not interested in hearing that you did not get paid. Your employees want to get their paychecks. Your prime contractor will tell you, "If we don't get paid, you don't get paid."

E. Staffing

Get the right employees. The first thing you look for are employees who are motivated, qualified, and have similar goals. I was blessed to have had very good employees who complemented my management skills. What should you look for in an employee or associate? Is he motivated? Is she analytical? Can they develop strategies that offer solutions? Do they have a balanced view? Can they be loyal to you and your clients?

We once had an employee who was in it for "self," and who we ultimately had to fire, which is one of the most intense confrontations a businessperson will encounter. Actually, we inherited the employee, and one of our project managers had a problem with him, so we kindly obliged by removing him from that project.

Even though there are no perfect employees and there are no perfect bosses, somehow you can get the work done.

Please be careful when considering hiring family members or friends to work with you. Remember that "friendship is friendship and business is business!"

F. Having The Right Tools

Get the services of an accountant, even if only on a consulting basis, to help you set up your books and records correctly from the start and determine the business structure. Ask for help in determining deductions so that you can plan your business expenses. Establish a routine for keeping strict records of all income and expenses right from day one. Keep all business-related receipts, invoices, client records, bank statements, bank deposit slips, and canceled checks.

As your business grows and you start bidding on larger contracts, an accountant will help you determine your company's multiplier, a formula used to calculate compensation based on direct salary cost, negotiated overhead expenses, and profit.

Work with your accountant to understand the steps to effectively manage and analyze your cash flow and learn how to best invest any profits. Maximizing cash flow is a priority for businesses of every size. But getting it right can be a challenge. A healthy cash flow is a requirement to survive.

You also will need a lawyer, a banker, and a mentor. The lawyer will help you with legal matters and contracts, a banker can help you establish a line of credit and help with your banking needs, and a mentor will guide you as you grow your business.

SECTION 4

Survival and growing your business

Chapter 4: Building Your Clients

Moving forward, our business continued to grow. The decade of the nineties was a good time to be in the public involvement business. Transportation agencies were placing more emphasis on making sure that all projects complied with the federal requirement to get public input from politicians, residents, business owners, community groups, and others to build consensus before approval. We were able to offer our services in English, Spanish, and Creole, as required, which was a big plus for us, since this was the beginning of the trend.

Running your own business and managing day-to-day operations is challenging. There is much to learn about human interaction with clients, project managers, other consultants, suppliers, staff, and others.

Running a business is all about constantly making decisions. Some decisions are wiser than others, but you can also learn from your mistakes.

The main tool of public involvement is communication. The process of public involvement is to develop two-way communications with the communities we serve. We used language that was easily understood by the public and not a lot of technical jargon.

To accomplish that, we conducted public meetings, workshops, and public hearings. Our audiences included politicians, appointed officials, residents, business owners, community groups, and many others.

We sent out mailings, produced collaterals, and placed advertisements in leading newspapers. Our goal was to demonstrate the feasibility and/or benefits of proposed projects.

Of course, it's commonly accepted that most people seldom read notices or attend meetings and only react when the cranes and bulldozers show up on their block to begin work on the project.

But the purpose of the meetings was to help make decisions as to whether to go forward, scale back, or drop a project. We usually presented recommendations and alternatives, and the consultants spent time brainstorming ideas, issues, and strategies, giving the public an opportunity to voice comments.

Some of the projects we handled were in the planning and design phase of long-range projects and others were actual construction projects.

We provided a full-time public information officer to work with the construction team, residents, businesses, community groups, and the driving public. We publicized detours, road closures, speed limits, bus stop and tree relocations, and driving safety information in construction zones. We provided signs for access to businesses and handled myriad other duties to communicate with the public and respond to their concerns.

Another important goal of public involvement is to make sure that perceptions do not become reality. Many times, rumors and innuendoes seem to run amok, and these can cause problems later on - or even doom a project. The role of public involvement is to put to rest all the rumors and innuendoes by providing factual and accurate information.

As our firm's reputation grew, so did our business. Our next step was to learn how to prepare proposals, make presentations, and win contracts.

The bidding process is very competitive and expensive. Some of the larger firms hire lobbyists. Some companies are successful in winning an award, and are challenged by their competition who will then file a bid protest . At this point the winning company will stand to lose the award and will have to incur fees for an attorney to argue their company's case. The process can take a long time and can become overburdened for all concerned.

At times even when you have a signed contract, you may not be completely out of the woods. For one reason or another the agency may decide to cancel all or part of the contract usually with no explanation.

So you learn not to count your chickens before they hatch. The only time to count your earnings is after the check has been deposited and cleared by the bank. Otherwise it is all guesswork.

We later had opportunities to work with several government entities on a variety of projects that helped us grow our business.

Chapter 5: The Value of Listening

Working with   the public over the years has taught us several things. We have learned to never underestimate the value of information received from others. They may know more than you think they do.

Listening is a fundamental part of the communication process. Regardless of the type of job you do or the industry in which you work, it is important to understand the listening process, have an awareness of barriers to listening effectively, and learn how to listen actively.

I remember working with the local electrical utility company on the expansion of its power lines through a predominantly black neighborhood. We surveyed residents and found they were very aware of the current issues related to substations and power lines, and the perceived health dangers of living in close proximity to such facilities.

Most people have a tendency to give more value to information from certain individuals and underestimate the value of information from others. At times, experts have a way of swaying our opinion, because we believe they know more than we do. But the truth is that, sometimes, they do not have all the facts. In addition, you must consider their values, their socio-economic background, and their experience with a similar problem.

The wiser you become about life and people the better a listener you will be. No matter your communication skills, if you don't have extensive wisdom about people, you will not come across as truly understanding them.

However, don't underestimate the value of information received from non-traditional groups, including low-income groups, women, the elderly, etc. Many times, they have a different perspective and can offer solutions.

I have learned, however, that some of the people who fight the hardest against projects have a vested interest and are seeking some kind of financial compensation. They are determined to sway or minimize the value of any solutions offered.

So, an important rule is that only hearing what you want to hear or seeing what you want to see can lead to erroneous decisions. If we have expectations or biases, we tend to see what we want to see.

Likewise, if someone tries to tell us something we do not want to hear, we simply do not hear him or her. This is a common mistake. We must practice the art of listening. There are no stupid, or insane ideas, just old ideas with a new twist. There are many groups of opinionated, paid hacksters and activists that make their money by selling their ideas at any rate.

The key is to be aware of your own prejudices and expectations, while at the same time, staying open and receptive to everything that comes your way. And last but not least, learn to follow your gut feelings. Most of the time your intuition will be right on target.

Another important secret to good listening is to train yourself to "listen" for clues of impending trouble or disaster. There is value in listening to the grapevine. It usually provides valuable information that can aid your survival. You need to know where the landmines are buried. What are the community's issues and sensitive points? Who are the people and what is fueling the fire? Remember every project has it's supporters and non-supporters, including politicians, lobbyist, environmentalists, activists and others who could Influence the final outcome.

The more you train yourself to "listen" for these subtle signs of trouble, the better you will appreciate what's going on. Listen for level of commitment, integrity, and sincerity.

Last but not least, the value of listening should apply to understanding your assignments as a consultant. Some assignments can be moving targets depending on the volatility of the project.

Make sure you understand the purpose of the assignment and its final goal. While discussing the assignment with your project manager It helps to take notes, writing down key words and phrases that will jog your memory later on. Ask questions and finally use the technique of repeating the task verbatim for further clarifications.

You should always strive to work closely with your project managers to provide the client with the best solutions to address the problems at hand. As a consultant your overall goal is to obtain support for the project and manage the expectations of stakeholders.

Chapter 6: Don't Burn Out: Learn To Delegate

Delegation is the assignment of authority and decision making to another person to carry out specific job-related activities. At the beginning, small-business owners try to do it all. It is understandable, because you have to be making money before you want to spend money on employees. Sometimes, I worked with independent contractors to avoid having to pay salaries or payroll taxes.

One of the ways as a manager to make the best use of your time and skills is to stop trying to do it all and learn to delegate. If you do this well, you can quickly build a strong team of people that can meet the demands of the business. This not only benefits you, but it also helps other people grow and develop to reach their full potential in the organization. This is why delegation is such an important skill and is one that you have to learn in order to succeed.

You should start by hiring people with the right background and credentials. When you assign a project, you should then spend time sharing project background, the tasks at hand, the deadlines, and your expectations. As project manager, you should always be available to answer questions or to help solve any problems that may arise. A memo confirming the discussions at the meeting should be prepared, including tasks, deadlines, and expectations. This leaves you with the responsibility of managing the contract, addressing contractual issues, preparing work plans, attending meetings, supervising staff, and preparing monthly billings, progress reports, and final reports. To determine when you should delegate, you should consider all or some of the following points:

- Is this a task that someone else can do, or is it critical that you do it yourself? What are your expectations or goals?

- Does the task provide an opportunity to grow and develop another person's skills?

- Do you have enough time to delegate the job effectively, and what are the consequences of not completing the job on time?

When you arrange the workload so that you, as the manager, are working on the high priority tasks and others on the staff are working on their assignments, you have a winning situation.

SECTION 5

Lessons learned: Government contracting

When I was running Gladys Kidd and Associates, opportunities moved us forward but challenges strengthened my resolve to succeed.

During the 1980s and '90s, in an effort to correct historic disparities, Miami-Dade County implemented a series of preference programs to create more diversity on the teams bidding for contracts.

The programs provided opportunities for blacks, Hispanics and women to compete and win county contracts. The results were significant. Under this program we formed several alliances with major primes seeking to compete for contracts and fulfill the new diversity requirements.

Similar versions of minority programs were being introduced nationwide. However, the programs were subsequently shut down because of many lawsuits. In 1997 the federal court found that Miami-Dade's minority programs were unconstitutional because the county had not demonstrated a pattern of discrimination.

The minority program was replaced with the Small Business Enterprise (SBE) program managed by the office of Small Business Development, in the Procurement Department.

Later we became certified as a Disadvantage Business Enterprise, (DBE), a federal designation that allowed us to work on transportation projects, which was our main source of business. We competed and managed projects as a prime contractor, in joint venture partnerships, and as sub-consultants.

The best part of being a sub-consultant on a major team is that you do not have to prepare the proposal, thus saving time and money. Proposal preparation requires a lot of research, writing and handling of paperwork so it is a blessing when you don't' have to do it. You only submit the required paperwork on your company.

We learned that the United States federal government was the biggest customer in the world, buying 20% of all the services and products produced in the U.S. But of the 22 million U.S. companies, less than 2% seek out this market.

I wanted to know why more small businesses were not tapping into this market? I learned that the reason is because small business owners don't know where and how to get these contracts.

I decided that learning to win government contracts was going to be our next challenge. We decided that in addition to local contracts we would pursue our 8a Business Development Certification to enable us to do business with the federal government.

This market today is growing for small and women-owned businesses.

Consider the following facts released by the SBA's Office of Advocacy in their 2010 Report on the Small Business Economy:

- Small businesses were awarded $96.8 billion in federal prime contracts in FY 2009, an increase of almost $4 billion from FY 2008.

- Small businesses increased their shares of contracting dollars by $1.5 billion to $4 billion from FY 2008 to FY 2009.

- Women owned small businesses were awarded $16.3 billion in 2009, up from $14.7 billion in 2008.

- Women owned and small business contracts increased 16.3 percent in 2009, from 14.7 percent in 2008.

Pursuing federal contracts through the 8a program was not an easy task. We bid unsuccessfully on several projects and learned very quickly that we had a lot to learn. The greatest aspect of our experiences was the debriefing sessions, which allowed the agency to share with us some of our shortcomings and explain why we did not win the award. We also had an opportunity to review the winning proposals, (except private and proprietary information), which taught us a lot. You have nine years to get it right and today the agency is a lot more user-friendly than in the early days. Finally, towards the end of our tenure we bid and were awarded a few contracts. I discuss my 8a experience further in chapter 10.

I compare the contracting experience to driving on a crowded superhighway. In the following section on lessons learned we have used road signs as markers to bring home the various points. The journey begins with you on the ramp trying to merge into heavy traffic. You have no previous driving experience, not even lessons. You must figure out how to stay in your lane, when to slow down, when to accelerate and when to slam on your brakes. Otherwise, you could end up stuck in a ditch while others are zooming along. Government contracting is a process. You must follow the road signs carefully to arrive safely to your destination.

I share some of my insights and experiences in playing the game. My hope is to enlighten you as to what could be in store if you decide to take a similar path. Remember that although businesses are different, and the players might change, the rules of the game are the same for everyone.

The game can be interesting and challenging, however if you succeed the rewards are great.

The following are several important lessons learned:

Chapter 7: Identifying And Managing Opportunities

LESSON LEARNED: THERE ARE MANY OPPORTUNITIES AVAILABLE FOR SMALL BUSINESSES TO GET GOVERNMENT CONTRACTS

Bid solicitations are the formal process used by official government agencies to obtain goods and services, including construction services or public works projects. Programs exist at the federal, state, and local level intended to increase the participation of minority owned businesses.

In addition many states, counties, and cities also have their own programs that may have set asides, bid preferences, focused outreach, or just set goals. These programs are typically called Minority Business Enterprise (MBE) or Minority or Women Business Enterprise (MWBE) programs.

State Departments of Transportation and local transit agencies have a goal for the participation of Disadvantaged Business Enterprises (DBE) for roadway and transportation infrastructure projects.

There are three main types of government procurement: open, selective and limited (or negotiated) procurement. In addition there are "informal" methods of procurement, such as Requests for Proposals and Requests for Quotations seeking detailed technical and cost proposals. RFQ generally means the same thing as Invitation to Bid, (ITB).

Bidders return a proposal by a set date and time. The proposals are used to evaluate the suitability of a supplier, vendor, or institutional partner. Discussion and evaluation of the proposals are held by an appointed screening committee.

Bidding on government contracts is a challenging and complex process to a novice, especially a small business lacking experience and financial resources. It is recommended that your firm be in business for several years before you take on this assignment because of the requirements of the bidding process. A lot of agencies provide training for new bidders.

If you are successful in winning a bid, it provides a good financial source to help build your business. These contracts are usually for larger amounts, are for multiple years and offer renewal options.

Chapter 8: Teaming Strategies: Selecting Partners

LESSON LEARNED: CHOOSE PARTNERS AND OTHER ALLIANCES CAREFULLY TO ASSURE SUCCESS.

For a small business there are various opportunities to bid on government contracts. You can bid as a prime contractor, you can form a joint venture or you can join a team as a sub-contractor in response to a bid requirements. In these days, government agencies want to "share the wealth" and look favorably on teaming as a method of doing that, rather than awarding to just one firm.

Prime Contractor

Bidding as a prime contractor is more involved and present special challenges to a small business with limited resources. As the chief or main contractor your firm assumes all the contractual responsibilities and risks. This means you put the team together, you write the proposal, prepare the presentation, file all the required paperwork, and organize and coordinate the presentation. After award of the contract, your firm manages the contract and works with the agency to negotiate the budget and carry out the terms of the contract. The prime also enjoys all the financial benefits.

Joint Venture Partnership

A joint venture is a new firm formed to achieve specific objectives of a partnership. A joint venture partnership brings together two or more firms to bid on a contract. It is often the best option for a small business with limited experience and resources. Joining forces with other firms offer opportunities to create a stronger entity. Collaboration brings together good energy, and can be a good alliance for a small business helping them to learn the rules of the game.

It is best to join forces with a larger, more established firm that can bring experience, and financial resources to the table. Other benefits of a joint venture, include diversity of team members, diversity of languages, broader experiences and contact base, and availability of a full staff to draw upon at any given time. Some of the downsides of the arrangement include differing philosophies, clashing egos of the partners, and inadequate compensation of partners.

Sub-Contractor Arrangement

This is the arrangement that holds the most possibilities for minority businesses. Joining a team as a sub-contractor is when you offer your services to a larger, prime contractor to fulfill the requirements of a bid package. In our case we were usually selected as a sub-contractor to fulfill the diversity issue and the team's public involvement requirements.

The team usually is comprised of various sub-contractors offering a variety of services to fit bid specifications. In this arrangement, the prime is responsible for putting the team together and handling the proposal and the sub-contractors submit their capabilities statement and fills out required paperwork.

After you have decided on a partner, make sure you get something in writing regarding the arrangement before you sign on. You need a contract or some type of written agreement that spells out the terms of the agreement, and the financial compensation. You should inquire what percentage of the contract will be allocated to your firm? Most government contracts require minority participation totaling around 15 to 20 percent of the total contract. The overall percentage is usually split among the minority firms on the team. Because public involvement was a required task, we usually fared very well. The downside of being a sub-contractor is that sometimes you are part of a team, but never get any work.

Chapter 9: Federal Contracts: Applying For 8a Certification

LESSON LEARNED: 8a CERTIFICATION LENDS CREDIBILITY AND CREATES OPPORTUNITY, BUT STRINGENT REQUIREMENTS ARE LIMITING.

An 8a certification is a Small Business Administration (SBA) designation that allows small businesses to compete for opportunities and set-asides with the federal government. The designation is good for nine years. The firm must be an established business and show experience in managing contracts and finances.

The U.S. federal government alone spends over $200 billion a year on goods and services. At the federal level, there are contract set-a-sides for companies certified under the Small Business Administration's 8(a) program, and also Small Disadvantaged Businesses (SDB).

Bidding and working with the federal government is a highly regulated process. For the novice there are many traps. The system is governed by a maze of statutes and regulations. The U.S. Government imposes a host of socio-economic obligations through its contracts, including requirements related to affirmative action, drug-free work place, subcontracting, and minimum employee wages.

Although Congress has streamlined the process to reduce the burdens on contractors, any firm considering entering into a government contract should tread carefully.

The following is the story of the challenges we faced trying to get our certification. However, the moral of our story is "don't let anyone tell you what you can and cannot do."

We started out by visiting the local office to make inquiries. The representative was not very encouraging, tried to discourage us, saying that it would be difficult, if not impossible, for our firm to become certified. We could not understand his response since we had been in business more than the required two years.

We left disappointed but determined to do some more research and prove him wrong. We proceeded to work with the SBA office in Washington, D. C., applied, filed all the paperwork and, ultimately received our certification.

Soon after that, we ran into the local SBA representative we had met with and we advised him of our success. He had the look of "a deer staring into the headlights." He knew that he had shrugged us off and had not done anything to assist us.

The same lack of assistance from the local people remained throughout the nine years of the certification. We did not get a lot of work from this effort, but we made some money at the end.

In retrospect, we realize that it was not the agency but the agency's representative, guarding the door, who chose not to provide the proper assistance. Remember these were the early days of the program and the rules were evolving and constantly changing. Today the SBA is very proactive in communicating and assisting small businesses. Their website is http://www.sba.gov

To be successful we also needed to have maintained a presence in Atlanta where the regional office is located, or in Washington, DC, the center of most federal activity.

I also learned that other firms use their political connections or hire lobbyists. I feel that most of these contracts are politically motivated. All in all, the challenge presented was a good learning experience.

Chapter 10: Negotiations

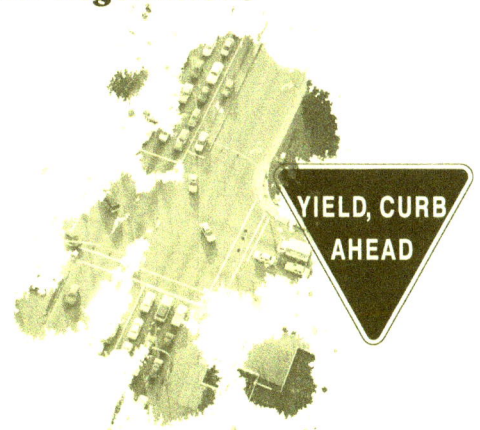

LESSON LEARNED: NEGOTIATING IS KEY TO FINANCIAL SUCCESS, BUT KNOW WHEN TO STAND FIRM AND WHEN TO YIELD.

Negotiating contracts can be intimidating, especially to a small-business owner. Clients always seem to want more work for less money.

One of the important functions that a small business must learn is to prepare a "scope of services," or a "work order" including an itemized budget consisting of the number of employees, number of hours per task, billable fees per task, and all expenses for which the contractor is to be held responsible.

Be accurate in estimating hours required to complete tasks. If a task takes longer than the hours allocated and approved, the consultant will not be paid for the extra hours. Some of the agencies use a schedule that indicates how many billable hours they allow per task.

In presenting your budgets or task orders during negotiations, it is important to remember that your fees are negotiable.

Chapter 11: Getting Paid

LESSON LEARNED: IT IS ONE THING TO HAVE THE CONTRACT BUT IT IS SOMETHING ELSE TO COLLECT.

Getting paid as a sub-consultant is a two-step process.
You submit invoices to the prime for work completed, invoices are reviewed for accuracy and then submitted for payment.

However, the wheels of bureaucracy are known to turn very slowly and it usually tends to take longer for payments to be processed, and for firms to receive payment. Established firms have more resources and can survive. But for small businesses with limited resources this can cause hardship or lead them to declare bankruptcy.

A situation that can delay payment of invoices is when the prime gets paid, but will not pay sub-consultants because of cash-flow problems. Also, you will not get paid if the prime has unresolved contractual issues with the agency. The agency is not responsible, nor does it arbitrate any disputes between the prime contractor and the sub-consultants. So, basically, if you encounter that situation you are on your own.

There is also the matter of "retainage" that requires that a certain percentage of your invoices be withheld to ensure a contractor will resolve unresolved problems. According to state law, government agencies can retain more than 10 percent of a contract amount until up to 50 percent of a project's completion, and allows for withholding 5 percent after that. The bottom line is that it can take several years before you are able to collect retainage fees.

Contracts usually have a prompt payment clause that says that payment shall be made in a timely manner, forty-five days, and that interest payments must be made on late payments. The reality is that most firms are never paid in forty-five days, nor do they receive interest payments on late invoices.

One of our worst offenders was a state transportation agency, that owed us over $120,000 for more than one year. The outstanding payment represented invoices for more than six months of work that included salaries, newspaper ads, printing and mailing expenses. We ended up subsidizing this agency which drained us of much needed resources.

Be prepared and pro-active when it comes to collecting your fees. Establish a reserve or a way to get funds to pay your bills.

Chapter 12: Marketing For Competitive Advantage

LESSON LEARNED: RELATIONSHIPS ARE EVERYTHING. IF THEY DON'T KNOW YOU, THEY DON'T NEED YOU!

Every business should start with a very good marketing strategy that makes it more competitive with other businesses in its field. It does not mean that larger businesses have more resources to start with. However, these businesses know how to maximize their resources and use them to their advantage. You must learn to do the same.

Marketing strategies are really about considering the resources available and finding creative ways to maximize them. It is not how many resources a business has at its disposal, but how creative they can get to make the resources work for them.

Some small business fear competing with bigger businesses that have more capital. However, if a business has a very good product, it can compete, provided it has prepared an effective marketing strategy for its business.

A marketing strategy is usually based on a goal. The strategy is implemented with the view of achieving something during a certain period. Each company must come up with different marketing strategies, depending on the products or services they provide. Some companies that have less capital can find a niche and then concentrate on dominating that niche.

Business owners should carefully plan their marketing strategies to keep their market presence strong. Your marketing plan should begin with research that answers some important questions, including these: Who are you targeting? Who is your competition? What are your present and potential markets?

We effectively marketed our firm to local and national architectural and engineering firms. I attended pre-bid conferences for major projects, workshops, networking meetings, and seminars. All of these gatherings offer opportunities to meet other players and build relationships that later can translate into contracts or at least good contacts. After the meeting, be sure to request a copy of the sign-in sheets. Here, you will find names of prime contractors who may be bidding and looking for the type of services your firm offers.

Prepare and mail marketing materials periodically to keep old clients up to date and to inform new clients as to the services you offer and your list of current clients. Spend a little more and prepare a color brochure or newsletter. It is so much more impressive.

The internet has become a very important part of our lives, and there are several options available to small businesses to showcase their products or services, including developing a website, e-mail marketing, and other online marketing programs.

Chapter 13: Preparing And Making Presentations

LESSON LEARNED: GREAT PRESENTATIONS WILL SET YOU APART FROM YOUR COMPETITION

Whether you're pitching a small client or you're part of a large team bidding on a contract, you will be required to make presentations.

The central purpose of any presentation - written, oral, or visual - is communication. To communicate effectively, you must state your facts in a simple, concise, and interesting manner.

Visuals should be used in support of the spoken or written word. A well-developed concept and effective script are the essential elements of any presentation. Hastily designed and produced visuals can doom a presentation. Images can add tremendous strength. PowerPoint presentations are usually good because they are easy to prepare and easy to make last-minute changes.

Finally, your presentation should be entertaining. Leave the audience feeling better.

A presentation consists of four basic elements: the presenter, your audience, your message, and your tools.

Here are the key steps:

- Know your subject matter.
- Know your audience.
- Know yourself.
- Develop a theme.
- Prepare your script.
- Select the proper visual aids.
- Prepare a storyboard.
- Produce the visuals.
- Rehearse, rehearse, rehearse.
- Make the presentation.

A word of caution: Make sure you have the right equipment and technicians to run the presentation. If your equipment fails to work at the last minute, you will be in big trouble. You can wing the presentation, but it will not be as effective.

The following is an example of a presentation I experienced, which was vivid, entertaining and memorable:

We worked as part of a lobbying team representing a client that owned a tourist attraction and sought to expand its recreational facilities to have more social events. Neighboring residents opposed the expansion citing traffic nightmares. Neighbors were tired of the tour buses in their neighborhood during the day and the thought of bus traffic during the evenings was the straw that broke the camel's back.

On the day of the hearing, the attorney representing the neighbors showed up at the county commission hearing with a large, green and red wooden bird. It might have been a cockatoo.

As he began his presentation, he placed the bird high up on the commission dais, high enough for all to see. He said that he had received it as a wedding gift, did not know what to do with it, and had been saving it for the right occasion.

The attorney opened his presentation by saying: "This bird won't fly." He followed with an eloquent argument in support of the neighbors opposing the project, because they felt that it would destroy their quality of life.

He was right. The bird did not fly and our client lost that round. The project did not get approved. But all that begins well ends well. Several years later the client relocated to a prime location downtown.

Chapter 14: Knowing Your Worth

LESSON LEARNED: DON'T TRY TO BE A WINNER IN A LOSING GAME. CHANGE DIRECTIONS

Several years ago, I was on the team of a large advertising agency competing for a $70 million, anti-tobacco contract, which resulted in the youth-oriented "truth" campaign. We signed on as the ad agency's minority partner and attended all of the meetings, including covering all the expenses associated with traveling for the final presentation. There were various steps to the evaluation process.

During the first evaluation session, we were questioned as to the team's diversity and why there were so few women and other minorities on the team. At the time mostly "white men" who headed the agency were on the team. There were two women on the team at that time, and together we made our case and convinced the committee that our team would be diverse.

After our final presentation in which I had a speaking role, we left feeling good about how things were proceeding. That afternoon it was announced that our team was the winning team.

In the days that followed that announcement, three African-American firms showed up, demanding to be included. The advertising agency at that point felt the pressure, took the money it had set aside for that marketing effort and threw it into a pond filled with the barracudas, and left it for them to sort out.

We gracefully resigned from that contract because we realized that the only "truth" was that the contract was highly political and that we were not being treated equitably as an original partner. We had actively participated and lent our support in winning the contract. We felt that the other firms had the same opportunity to join a team and compete. Instead, they stood on the sidelines, waiting to get the spoils after we had killed the prey.

So we wrote the ad agency a "dear john" letter, saying, "Sorry, we hate to go." We never requested reimbursement for our expenses, because I firmly believe that you must pay for your learning experience.

After our resignation, I received many calls asking us to reconsider our decision because we were such "valuable members" of the team. I never responded, but thought, "You should have treated us more like valuable members of the team."

Chapter 15: Document, Document, Document

LESSON LEARNED: IF IT IS NOT IN WRITING, IT DOES NOT EXIST

Another important rule is to document, document, document. Even if you have a simple conversation about an issue that could come back to haunt you, write a "memo to file," documenting the conversation. In other cases, you can send a memo or e-mail to the parties concerned, confirming the substance of the conversation.

Our firm had a contract with a large, national media company that sold advertising at the airport. After we signed our contract which was very general, the prime's interpretation was that we were expected to sell advertising, and we would only be paid commission based on sales.

As a small company, we could not afford to pay an employee to sell advertising with the hopes that we would collect a commission based on sales. In addition, we were expected to compete with the prime's well trained and experienced New York sales force, which had all the accounts locked up.

This arrangement had no benefits to our bottom line in any way. We went back and forth with our small-business representative at the airport, who was there to assist us. We had traded memos and other paperwork for one-year in an attempt to negotiate a more equitable contract. The real problem here is that it was the first contract of this type at the airport, so they allowed the fox to guard the henhouse.

After several meetings and conversations with the airport contractor and the airport representatives, a meeting was called to address our concerns and to work out a new arrangement. I showed up at the meeting with my documentation: a two-page cover letter, plus attachments "a" through "z", as part of our argument. When the prime realized the level of my documentation, they tried to solve the problem by providing us with a "memo of understanding" to address our concerns.

It took several years to get to a place where we could make some money on this contract. I sold a few spots so some money was coming in. But considering that this was a multi-million dollar contract there was very little money in it for the minority partners. But, had we not had proper documentation, we probably would have made zero.

Chapter 16: Unexpected Assignments

LESSON LEARNED: CUSTOMER SERVICE IS EVERYTHING. EXPECT THE UNEXPECTED AND BE PREPARED TO ANSWER THE CALL

You also must be prepared to handle surprises, (assignments outside of your scope of services), when fulfilling your contractual duties.

Once while working as a sub-consultant under a miscellaneous contract for one of the county attractions, we were asked to handle the bid-solicitation process to hire an architectural and engineering firm to replace one that had been fired for default.

Our firm had never handled a bid solicitation, but were familiar with the process because of our prior experience bidding on contracts.

We advertised the bid and conducted the presentation and evaluation process for selection of the consultant. The process was tedious and time consuming, since more than half a dozen firms applied for the contract. The bid solicitation was completed to the satisfaction of all concerned. We also learned that eliminating the bureaucracy makes things go a lot faster. A task that traditionally takes between six and nine months to complete was done in less than three months.

SECTION 6

Turning fear into action: Be true to what you believe in

So I have offered tips on starting and operating your business and discussed some of the pros and cons of doing business with the government. But there is still a major lesson to be learned:

Follow your bliss and turn your fears into action. You must be true to what you believe in.

Over the years, I have experienced the good, the bad, and the ugly as a business owner but there is no better game than being an entrepreneur and creating your own destiny. Against all the odds, the political climate, the games that people play, I had the opportunity to play big as a small business and live the American dream.

I broke all the rules. I did not meet with community leaders, did not lobby politicians, did not hire lobbyists, but conducted my business the professional way, utilizing the tools and lessons learned throughout my career. For people with no connections, no history, and no money, it can be hard to survive and succeed in business.

But today is a new day. Many more small businesses are carving out their piece of the economic pie following the examples of others that preceded them. There are opportunities for people who want to be their own boss and chart their own future.

Remember you will never accumulate any wealth, working for someone else. If you are prepared, have skills, drive, and passion, you can achieve success in running your own business.

I want my experience to be a lesson to other people, helping them to master this thing called life. Don't be afraid of failure. Failure can be a great teacher. Failure and the fear of it can cripple you or make you settle for less. Instead put on your positive hat, wear it proudly and overcome your fears. Follow through on your dreams, and you will become the best that you can be.

SECTION 7

Inspirations

I have selected several motivational quotes to share with you, designed to inspire you with confidence and optimism.

"Don't limit yourself. Many people limit themselves to what they think they can do. You can go as far as your mind lets you. What you believe, remember, you can achieve."
   —Mary Kay Ash

"Learn from the mistakes of others. You can't live long enough to make them all yourself."
   —Eleanor Roosevelt

"I believe through learning and application of what you learn, you can solve any problem, overcome any obstacle, and achieve any goal that you can set for yourself."
   —Brian Tracy

"You have to think anyway, so why not think big?"
   —Donald Trump

"The victory of success is half won when one gains the habit of setting goals and achieving them. Even the most tedious chore will become endurable as you parade through each day convinced that every task, no matter how menial or boring, brings you closer to fulfilling your dreams."
   —Og Mandino

"Part of the issue of achievement is to be able to set realistic goals,

but that's one of the hardest things to do because you don't always know exactly where you're going, and you shouldn't."
 —George Lucas

"The three great essentials to achieve anything worthwhile are, first, hard work; second, stick-to-itiveness; third, common sense."
 —Thomas Edison

"Speech has allowed the communication of ideas, enabling human beings to work together to build the impossible. Mankind's greatest achievements have come about by talking, and its greatest failures by not talking. It doesn't have to be like this. Our greatest hopes could become reality in the future. With the technology at our disposal, the possibilities are unbounded. All we need to do is make sure we keep talking."
 —Stephen Hawking

"A leader has the vision and conviction that a dream can be achieved. He inspires the power and energy to get it done."
 —Ralph Nader

"You must master your time rather than becoming a slave to the constant flow of events and demands on your time. And you must organize your life to achieve balance, harmony, and inner peace."
 —Brian Tracy

"Defeat is not the worst of failures. Not to have tried is the true failure."
 —George Edward Woodberry

"Develop success from failures. Discouragement and failure are two of the surest stepping stones to success."
 —Dale Carnegie

"Failure is success if we learn from it. "
 —Malcolm Forbes

"Don't aim for success if you want it; just do what you love and believe, and it will come naturally."
   —David Frost

"I don't know the key to success, but the key to failure is trying to please everybody."
   —Bill Cosby

"Your ability to negotiate, communicate, influence, and persuade others to do things is absolutely indispensable to everything you accomplish in life. The most effective men and women in every area are those who can quite competently organize the cooperation and assistance of other people toward the accomplishment of important goals and objectives."
   —Brian Tracy

"Leaders are made, they are not born. They are made by hard effort, which is the price which all of us must pay to achieve any goal that is worthwhile."
   —Vince Lombardi

""Every man and woman is born into the world to do something unique and something distinctive and if he or she does not do it, it will never be done."
   —Dr. Benjamin E. Mays, Former President of Morehouse
      College

SECTION 8

Small business resources

SMALL BUSINESS ADMINISTRATION

http://www.sba.gov

SBA App - New device that helps users connect with SBA district office staff and SBA affiliated counselors and mentors who can provide free personalized small business assistance. The app will first be available for the Apple iPhone, with future versions for other platforms. Source: Miami Herald Business section

SMALL BUSINESS DEVELOPMENT CENTER

http://www.sba.gov/content/small-business-development-centers-sbdcs

SCORE

http://www.score.org

EXPORT ASSISTANCE CENTER

http://www.export.gov

SECTION 9

Glossary for small businesses: Terms relevant to starting a business

Accrual basis accounting. An accounting method that records sales, expenses or other events at the time they occur, rather than when cash changes hands.

Amortization. The gradual payment of a debt through a schedule of payments or the writing off of an intangible asset against expenses over the period of its useful life.

Articles of Incorporation. A document filed with the secretary of state of a state which sets forth certain required information about the corporation.

Balance sheet. A listing of a company's assets, liabilities and net worth as of a fixed point in time.

Board of Directors. A group of individuals, elected by the shareholders of a company, who oversee the management of the company.

Break-even analysis. The method of determining the exact point at which a company makes neither a profit nor a loss.

Business plan. A written document that describes a business, its objectives, strategies, market and financial forecast.

Capital. Monies invested in a business enterprise.

Cash basis accounting. An accounting method that records sales and expenses when the transfer of cash occurs.

Cash flow statement. A charting of sources and uses of cash of a business.

Certificate of Incorporation. A certificate issued by the secretary of state of a state indicating that a company's articles of incorporation have been accepted for filing and that the company is incorporated.

Collateral. Business or personal property that a borrower pledges to a lender as security to ensure repayment of a loan.

Corporation. An organization formed under state law for the purpose of carrying on a business enterprise is such a manner as to make the enterprise distinct from its owners.

Current assets. Assets of a business that can be liquidated within a relatively short period of time.

Current liabilities. Debts that must be paid within a relatively short period of time, usually within one year.

Current ratio. A ratio of a business' current assets to its current liabilities.

Debt financing. The use of borrowed money to finance a business.

Depreciation. The process of expensing the value of a business asset over its useful life.

Equity. The net value of assets minus liabilities.

Equity financing. The securing of a monetary investment from an investor in which the investor becomes a part owner of the business.

Fiscal year. The twelve-month period established by a business for accounting, planning and tax purposes.

Financial reports. Reports that show the financial status of a company at a given time.

Financial statement. A presentation of financial information derived from the accounting records.

Financial statements include a Balance Sheet, Income Statement (or Profit and Loss Statement), and Cash Flow Statement.

Fixed costs. Business costs that do not vary with sales volume.

Forecasting. The calculation of reasonable probabilities about a business' financial future.

Goodwill. An intangible asset of a business derived from the perceived value of the business' assets.

Gross profit. Net sales minus the cost of goods sold.

Guaranty. A promise by a third party to repay a loan in the event the primary borrower fails to do so.

Income statement. A presentation of the sales, expenses, and profit or loss of a business on a periodic basis.

Intangible asset. An asset that does not have a physical presence, such as goodwill, a patent or a trademark.

Inventory financing. The process of obtaining capital for a business by borrowing money with inventory used as collateral.

Joint venture. An agreement between two or more businesses to mutually accomplish a business objective.

Leverage. The use of borrowing to increase the ability of a business to conduct its operations.

Limited liability company. An organization, distinct from a corporation, formed under state law for the purpose of carrying on a business enterprise is such a manner as to make the enterprise distinct from its owners.

Line of credit. A commitment by a lender to lend up to a certain amount of money to a business.

Net profit after taxes. A company's net profit before taxes, minus federal, state or local income or franchise taxes.

Net profit before taxes. Net sales or total receipts of a business minus all expenses except taxes.

Net sales. Total sales of a business minus discounts, returns and pricing adjustments.

Net worth. The net value of assets minus liabilities.

Operating expenses. The expenses of a business not directly associated with the making of a product or providing of a service, such as administrative, technical or selling expenses.

Partnership. An association of two or more persons to carry on as co-owners of a business for profit.

Public offering. The sale by a company of shares of its stock to the public in the financial market.

Sole proprietorship. A business that is owned and operated by an individual owner without incorporation or partners. The owner is liable for the business' debts to the full extent of his or her personal property.

Subchapter S corporation. A corporation that has elected under Subchapter S of the Internal Revenue Code not to pay any corporate taxes on its earnings, and instead to have its shareholders pay taxes on it.

Retained earnings. Net profit after taxes that is retained in the business as working capital.

Securities and Exchange Commission. The federal governmental agency that maintains order of the stock and securities exchanges.

Small Business Administration. The federal governmental agency that guarantees loans made by banks to small businesses.

Unsecured loan. A loan made with no collateral posted to ensure repayment.

Variable cost. A cost that varies directly with sales, such as raw materials, labor and sales commissions.

Working capital. Current assets minus current liabilities.

WHY THE NEED FOR THIS BOOK?

The United States federal government is the biggest customer in the world. It buys 20% of all the services and products produced in the U.S. Yet, of the 22 million registered U.S. companies, fewer than 2% of them seek out this market. Small business owners don't seek out this market because they don't know where and how to get government contracts.

This information can change that!

www.ingramcontent.com/pod-product-compliance
Lightning Source LLC
Chambersburg PA
CBHW051336170526
45166CB00002B/836